SELL YOURSELF
SHORT!

SELL YOURSELF
SHORT!

What on earth is the stock market?
For entrepreneurs

Firyal Hussain

PARTRIDGE

Print information available on the last page.

To order additional copies of this book, contact
Toll Free 0800 990 914 (South Africa)
+44 20 3014 3997 (outside South Africa)
orders.africa@partridgepublishing.com

www.partridgepublishing.com/africa

CONTENTS

DEDICATION

For the Non-Conformists;
The Seasoned Dreamers;
To the Light Searchers;
For Those-Who-Dig-for-Gold;
And for My Husband,
My Best Friend,
My Hero

ACKNOWLEDGEMENTS

Without being too fluffy and trying not to throw glitter all over the place, I would like to mention my heartfelt thanks to:

Ryan Hoover –

For taking me under your wing and helping me to grow without asking for anything in return

For reading my piece before it was even a thought of a book to be published

For being a giant on whose shoulders I could climb

And take a look at the view.

Siphiwe Dondolo –

For being ever enthusiastic about everything – EVER-RY-THING

For reading my book with lightning speed

For noticing my entrepreneurial spirit from the look in my eye and not from anything I had said to you

You have motivated me in ways you will never know how.

Muhammed Sheik -

> For reviewing my book end-to-end and forking out the grammatical errors by the truck load
> For being my brother, my friend and for being that person I can always look up to
> I still want to be just like you.

Dwaine van Vuuren –

> For allowing me to use the information from Sharenet.com
> For the assistance in making the book better and more useful to those who will benefit from reading it
> For being exceptionally awesome!

Johann du Preez –

> For allowing me to use the screenshots depicting share movements from Sharedata.
> My humble appreciation for supporting me in my venture.

My Foaad –

> For loving me the way the moon loves the ocean
> For being my window when get I locked inside my own head
> For smiling when the world is stripping us of everything we think we know
> For whispering sweet encouragements
> For making this book possible – in the eye of our storm ☺

"Who said it could not be done? And what great victories has he to his credit which qualify him to judge others accurately?"

Napoleon Hill

PREFACE

Why should you read this book?

Every reader will have a different objective for wanting to learn more about the stock market:

1. A student may want to know if this is a field that they would enjoy studying in future
2. A business person may want more tools at his/her disposal to better analyse the economic climate – what can the data provided by the stock market tell me?
3. A working mother may want to learn more about investing on the market but needs an introduction thereto
4. Someone may want to be able to hold a conversation about the stock market
5. Perhaps you would simply like to learn something new

Whatever your intention is, use this introductory book as a springboard.

Why have I written this book?

I wanted to teach those who have limited or no knowledge of the stock market, about the stock market.

I have chosen to do this from the angle of tutoring an entrepreneur because unlike any other profession, there is no concrete education foundation that will determine your success/failure as an entrepreneur. It comes from the spirit inside you.

Therefore, you do not have to have a Finance or Engineering degree to understand the concepts and examples used in this text. You just have to be you.

How should you use this book?

Guideline 1 – Don't view the book as work, it is not a textbook that you need to study.

Guideline 2 – Because this book is not meant to be work, try reading it when you are relaxed – before bed, while eating lunch alone, while on the train. This way you are more likely to soak it up.

Guideline 3 – Try not to read everything at once. This book is densely packed with facts and concepts that are important to grasp – so take your time and read a section more than once if you feel like you did not fully understand it the first time.

Guideline 4 – Everything is difficult before it is easy. Refer back to the content as much as you like once you have completed reading it.

Guideline 5 – Implement further actions to deepen your knowledge of the stock market if you so wish.

INTRODUCTION

Why do we need a separate book describing the stock market for entrepreneurs?

We will look at 3 examples to assist in answering this question:

1. Specimen X

    Specimen X has a degree in something fancy and has slotted in nicely halfway up the corporate ladder of a multinational company. Five years down the line she has moved a few small molehills and now has a steady job – that pays very well.

    X does not work from 8 to 5. She is allowed to work from 7 to 3:30 and gets to beat the traffic!

    X loves to be challenged and she has made a promise to herself that when boredom starts to set in she will apply for a more ambitious job where she will perhaps be the manager and can finally start delegating! Whoop, whoop!

    Life is all about choices and X has made all the right ones. Her reward?

    She is happy.

2. Specimen Y

Specimen Y also has a degree in something fancy. Specimen Y also starts at the mid-rung of the corporate ladder at a multinational company. She quickly learns that something is wrong with her.

After an uncomfortable stay, Y jumps ship and finds a new job with more pay, better benefits and a higher status. The new job is both challenging and demanding. But something is still wrong…

- Specimen Y begins to develop chest pains
- She misses seeing the sky for the greater part of the day
- She finds something wrong with apologizing for being ill/having to attend to family responsibilities
- Every millisecond sucks more life out of her
- Her cubicle begins to feel like her grave that she digs deeper into. Every. Single. Day.

She puts in a month's notice and begins to freelance so that she may see more of the sky.

3. Specimen Z

Z's education history is not important. He has never been an employee in all his life. He started doing business when – well, we cannot really pinpoint when he actually STARTED making money.

Z has a mind of his own and now heads a successful suburban agriculture company (he helps city slickers grow vegetable gardens on their balconies – he believes strongly in organic nutrition). He also runs a bread subscription service that delivers bread and milk to peoples' homes that do not want the inconvenience of stopping at the garage after work (rather than stand in a queue at the local supermarket).

"Bread should not cost this much for convenience sake" is what his company claims.

Analysis:

Almost everyone you meet will have similarities to Specimen X. The education history is irrelevant in this analogy. Most people are content with a day-job complete with job description and detailed duties and responsibilities. They are content within defined perimeters. Stability is what matters.

There are many books out there on investing advice for Specimen X.

Think about it this way, suppose you walk into a store on earth wanting to try on some hats. The hats say one-size-fits-all. This is okay if you are from earth. Not if you are an alien from planet K26015 v6 with a head the size of the average watermelon.

In much the same way, the level of understanding of the stock market and the type of investment opportunities are different for employees when compared to entrepreneurs. Here are just some of the differences:

Legend:
Employee = someone who intends to work for somebody else until retirement age
Entrepreneur = not someone defined as an employee. Not a bum either.

	Employee	Entrepreneur
Income amount	Limited, constant monthly amount with annual increases and a possible bonus	Unlimited, varies month on month
Risk appetite	Moderate to low risk	Very high risk appetite
Ability to identify opportunity	Perhaps	Finely tuned opportunity identification machine
Willingness to learn	I will learn it if is going to further my career	Insatiable
Information consumption habits	Driven by interests	Time is precious, information consumed on a need-to-know basis
Time spent travelling the road less travelled	Great holidays!	I don't know what I am actually doing, so I guess I am still on this road

The point that I am making here is that what is out there may not be information that should be consumed for your purposes – that is to understand what the stock market is, what it means for the economy (and thereby your business) and to potentially wet an appetite for the ocean of possibilities that it presents for cowboys (like you) who are willing to hunt.

So what is the stock market?

Here is an overview of what this section of the book aims to reveal in simple English:

I know that it sounds excruciatingly boring but I will try to make it as applicable to real life as my imagination can muster.

1. Chapter 1: What is a share?

2. Chapter 2: What are the 2 main types of companies in South Africa?

3. Chapter 3: The stock market – Company perspective

   a) Who can list on the stock exchange?
   b) Why would a company want to list on the stock exchange?
   c) What are the requirements for listing on the stock exchange? (You may want to read this one just before bed)
   d) How does one list on the stock exchange? (If you are still awake, read this one, you will definitely fall asleep)

4. Chapter 4: The stock market – Investor perspective

   a) Buying and selling of shares introduction
   b) Caution, red light ahead
   c) Why does a share have value and why does the value fluctuate? - growth in company, inflation, speculative growth
   d) How does investing in shares actually grow your money?
   e) Let's look at how to read the everyday stock market data
   f) Is the stock market a reflection of the economy?
   g) What costs are involved buying and selling shares? (remember what I said – *need-to-know basis*)
   h) As an entrepreneur, how does this apply to you?

5. Chapter 5: Closing

<u>Short Glossary</u>

- "Stock market" and "Stock exchange" mean the same thing. It refers to a platform which allows the purchase and sale of shares - such as the Johannesburg Stock Exchange.

- Shares, stocks and equities in this book all mean the same thing. It refers to the shares which are being bought and sold on the stock exchange.

CHAPTER 1

What is a share?

"I am a better investor because I am a businessman and a better businessman because I am an investor."

Warren Buffett

Explanation of a share

The best explanation I have come across for this question was an answer from Ryan Hoover on his website http://investinginafrica.net/,

"Owning a share means that you own a little piece of a company."

The technical way of explaining a share would be to say that you own the value of assets minus liabilities in proportion to the percentage of shares that you hold (you are entitled to the equity).

But what on earth does that mean?

Let's take a hypothetical company example – Ping (Pty) Ltd

Ping is a company that manufactures and sells ping pong balls to large distributors. It has been doing badly for the past 3 years.

There are 10 investors, each owning one share in Ping. We call these people *shareholders*.

Ping goes bust on the 25th August 2016 and the liquidator has to sell off the assets in order to pay off the company's creditors and loans.

After all the liabilities have been paid, there is a total of R1,000 in assets left over.

This R1,000 now needs to be shared amongst the shareholders.

This means that each of the 10 shareholders will be given R100 – each.

Here are the numbers again:

On the 25th Aug 2016, the company owned the following assets	20,000
On the 25th Aug 2016, the company had liabilities amounting to the following	(18,000)

The liquidator sells all the assets and uses that money to pay all the liabilities:

Remainder after settling liabilities (equity value)	2,000
Liquidator fees (purely hypothetical, lol)	1,000
Amount left for shareholders to *share*	1,000
Amount given to each of the 10 *shareholders*	100

What is a company?

Limited liability

A company is a business vehicle that enjoys *limited liability*.

This means that as a shareholder, you can only lose the amount that you paid for your shares.

Let's go back to our company Ping (Pty) Ltd.

Mr. Shabalala bought one share in Ping. He paid R50 for this share.

On the 25th Aug 2016 when Ping went bust, if the liabilities were R25,000 and the assets were R20,000; the creditors could not come and claim the outstanding R5,000 from Mr. Shabalala and his fellow shareholders.

In the event that the liabilities were R25,000 and the assets were R20,000; there would be no residual for the shareholders. Mr Shabalala would lose his initial investment of R50 – he would lose no more. This is what limited liability means.

The creditors will have to write off the remaining R5,000 outstanding amount as a bad debt.

CHAPTER 2

―――✦―――

What are the 2 main types of companies in South Africa?

"An investment in knowledge pays the best interest."

Benjamin Franklin

There are 2 main types of companies in South Africa:

1. Private company
2. Public company

Both have limited liability and both are governed by the Companies Act 2008 with amendments.

There are other types of companies but we will not explore these here.

The main difference between a private company and a public company is the way in which they are allowed to sell their shares.

Public companies can make an offering to the public (that is to you and I) to purchase shares in their company. A private company is not allowed to do this.

It is by virtue of this difference between the 2 types of companies that only public companies are allowed to sell and have their shares traded on the stock market or stock exchange.

CHAPTER 3

The stock market –
Company perspective

"Know what you own, and know why you own it."

Peter Lynch

a) Who can list on the stock exchange?

Only public companies are allowed to list on the stock exchange. If a private company wants to raise more capital, they will first need to convert the company into a public company before trying to list on the stock exchange to raise the required capital.

b) Why would a company want to list on the stock exchange?

To cut a long story short, a company would *list* on the stock exchange for prestige and in order to raise more capital. There are more reasons – which lead to the same concept of prestige and needing large amounts of money.

Companies would need large amounts of money to implement strategic plans and new developments. For example, a clothing outlet may want to convert itself into a fully digital store to cater for the emerging e-commerce market.

c) What are the requirements for listing on the stock exchange?

There are a host of requirements before a company can list on the stock market. The requirements for different stock markets around the world will vary. The reason we have listing requirements is to ensure the quality of the companies which list on the stock exchange.

Here are the main listing requirements for the JSE:

Please note that if you are imminently going to list on the stock exchange, do not use this list as it has been purposefully and stringently condensed with the intention of keeping both of our enthusiasm alive.

Listing requirements JSE

These requirements are imposed by the JSE over and above the requirements imposed by the Companies Act:

1. **Size** - Subscribed capital of at least R25,000,000 with a minimum of 25,000,000 shares in issue
2. 3 years **audited financials**
3. The most recent audit must have had R8million before tax profit (and other adjustments not worth mentioning here)
4. 20% of each class of equity share **held by the public**
5. **Financial reporting standards** requirements
6. **Corporate governance** requirements
7. Compliance with **Companies Act**

I am proceeding to go for a walk around the house and possibly wretch in the bathroom after writing this, you may want to do the same after reading it.

d) How does one list on the stock exchange?

Before listing on the JSE for example, a public company needs to have 20% of its shares already held by the public.

Therefore, at a minimum, 80% of the shares would most probably still be owned by the original owners.

After meeting the listing requirements – the action of actually *listing on the stock exchange* includes an activity called an IPO – *Initial Public Offering*. An IPO is necessary to allow for the shares of the company to *float* in the public. It is when the company sells its shares to the public for the very. First. Time.

This means that you and I can purchase shares of a company through the IPO of that company if it is listing for the first time.

After the IPO, a large amount of shares will be owned by the public (you and I) and can therefore be traded (I can sell my shares which I purchased to another person who wishes to buy them).

The IPO raises a large amount of money for the company in the process which the company can use to invest in their development.

It is an enormous decision for a company to list on a stock exchange and this decision should never be taken lightly. In addition to operating in the public eye, the company has additional reporting, disclosure and regulatory requirements which it needs to be prepared to comply with.

CHAPTER 4

The stock market – Investor perspective

"How many millionaires do you know who have become wealthy by investing in savings accounts? I rest my case."

Robert G. Allen

Now that you understand what the stock market represents for large companies, let's have a look at what the JSE for example, represents for you.

a) Buying and selling of shares introduction

Technology has expanded our world in terms of access to resources. Today, I can pay and attend a Harvard course online from the comfort of my own home in Johannesburg, South Africa. I can stream the Liverpool Manchester game at 10 at night and I have the ability to invest in the shares of world class companies.

The ability to invest in the shares is coupled with the avalanche of information that you have access to in terms of these stocks.

In 2014, JSE information was made available on Google Finance. Google Finance allows for share information to be more widely available - not only for the benefit of us here in South Africa but also globally which could help encourage foreign investment on the JSE.

Note on Google Finance – what can you do with Google finance?

If you are a still a start-up investor and cannot yet afford a trading account (or you don't even have money to invest in shares yet), Google Finance provides the perfect minefield ready for gold discovery:

1. You can create a share portfolio including all the companies you would possibly want invest in and track their progress
2. You can view the performance of a specific share over a period of time
3. You can read up on your shares' articles and news
4. And more!!!

Google Finance share prices are provided with a 15 minute delay. Despite the hype of "live share prices", if you are not going to sell the shares 3 hours after purchasing it (which you are not), the importance of live prices becomes less relevant.

Once you register on a platform where you can now buy shares, the platform you use to trade in shares would provide you with share information – for example if you have a share trading account with a bank, you will have access to live share information.

Gone are the disgusting days when you had to have a certain amount of money (particularly exorbitant to exclude a whole class of people) saved up before you could get within a 500 meter radius of a stockbroker.

It does not matter whether you are rich or busying yourself trying to get rich – you can buy shares!

Why would an entrepreneur want to buy shares?

Entrepreneurs are an anomaly. Whereas the majority of the population would opt for the safe option, you choose the unconventional;

1. Entrepreneurs by nature do not conform
2. Contrary to popular belief, entrepreneurs are not driven by money
3. As mentioned before, your risk appetite is unparalleled
4. You learn more, faster. Because you have to stay ahead of the curve
5. Entrepreneurs have a vital skill which is being applied in business - opportunity identification

The fact that you go against the grain, you are not driven purely by money, you love learning, you have an impressive risk threshold, you learn efficiently and you can identify opportunity makes you an unusual investor.

As is always the case with business, you can fail or you can win BIG.

b) Caution - red light ahead

There are many books out there which claim instant or guaranteed riches. I do not here aim to discredit their methods;

I simply want you to be vigilant and alert when you come across these works.

Remember that, like in business, you can tick all the boxes but it may not work out. You may be broke within the next 6 months. I feel like the books which promise riches mainly do so to increase sales figures and not to improve your knowledge of the stock market and how to analyse shares.

"…the future will always surprise us – always!"
Graham Benjamin

Training yourself takes time because you will be learning a new skill. Once you start getting your hands dirty (even if this is only on a dummy account) you will develop a knack for what works for you and what doesn't.

You can actually start getting your hands dirty right now using Google Finance and creating a watchlist for yourself of companies that you find to be suitable for observation. You can track the value of these shares over a period of time as if you own them and see what analytical methods work best for you.

My point is, be careful what you feed your mind because it affects your thoughts. If trained and seasoned stock pickers can get it wrong, it proves that there are no golden trusted methods. Your bet is as good as mine ☺.

c) Why does a share have value and why does the value fluctuate?

Let's take an example to demonstrate this.

Say for example that you own 100 shares in a well-known telecommunication company. How is it that this share actually has value?

There are 3 factors which contribute to the value of a share:

i)   Growth in business
ii) Inflation
iii) Speculative growth

Each of these in turn:

i)   *Growth in business*
Growth in the actual business itself would increase the value of your shares. As the company's profits rise year on year, the equity value of the company increases and thereby so does the value of your shares!

ii) *Inflation*
Inflation is the general rise in prices. Inflation within a defined range is good because it represents a healthy economy.

Research shows that with healthy inflation, companies generally do better.

When inflation is too low, company results are generally poor.

High inflation causes volatile company results and is difficult to predict.

iii) *Speculative growth*
Speculation in simple terms means "what do I think is going to happen in the future?". This sentiment increases/

decreases the demand for different shares on the stock market. Speculation is affected by information – this can come in many forms such as an article on a specific company or the reporting of quarterly results of a company.

Example of an article that could affect share price – positive impact:

Company A is in the pharmaceutical industry and is a listed company on the JSE. Company A announces interest in purchasing Company Q (a non-listed company). Company Q's research involving new methods of treating cancer have come to a standstill due to a lack of capital investment. Company A intends to pump Company Q with sufficient resources to further its study for the new treatment of cancer.

The markets react positively to the announcement made by Company A and rush off to buy shares in the Company A as they believe that the share price is going to go up should Company A successfully purchase Company Q. They believe that the operations of the 2 companies combined is good news and will enhance profitability.

Result: There is an increase in demand for Company A's shares. This drives up the price of Company A's shares on the stock exchange.

It is important to note that nothing has actually happened yet. Company A is in no better position after the announcement that it was before the announcement because it has not yet purchased Company Q. There has been no increase in the profit of Company A – its actual operations have not altered.

The increase in share price is solely due to *speculation* (this can also be called *investor sentiment*). Investors reading the article believe that the announcement is good news and will result in positive profits for Company A in the *future*. This information has increased demand for the shares of Company A, thereby driving up the share price.

<u>*Example of company results that could affect share price – negative impact:*</u>

Company C is in the automobile industry. It has been a trying 3 months and Company C is to report quarterly results within the next 24 hours.

24 hours passes and Company C reports a quarterly net loss of R7.64 million.

Result: There is a decrease in demand for Company C's shares. This causes the share price of Company C to decrease.

Negative results have caused investors to speculate that Company C will not do well in the future - *speculation*. Investors sell off their shares in Company C to prevent further losses to their share portfolio in the form of a decreased share price.

The reporting of negative results has caused investors to view the company in a bad light and thereby causing them to sell off their shares in the company. Since demand for the share is low, the share price decreases. The information reported by Company C has decreased demand for shares in Company C and thereby reducing the overall share price.

<u>*Other examples that could affect share price:*</u>

Note that there are many other factors which could affect the demand for shares. For example negative rumours about a specific sector such as the mining industry in South Africa; it could be changes in regulation which could affect a specific industry; there could be bad publicity for a company – such as a major reported oil spill or dangerous cars being sold to consumers.

Practical example of the impact of demand on price – a slight breather:

If you are unfamiliar with the concept of the impact of increase/decrease in demand on price, have a look at the below example:

Price of swimsuits at the approach of winter

The price of a swimsuit in summer is significantly higher than it is in winter. In fact, as soon as winter starts creeping in the price of swimsuits plummet!

This is because there is no need for a swimsuit in winter (low demand).

Clothing outlets therefore have to reduce the price come winter if they want any possibility of getting it off the shelves and into your wardrobe.

Low demand = lower price

On the other hand, as soon as winter starts the price of boots soars. The effect of the approach of winter on boots is the direct opposite of what happens to swimsuits. Demand for boots increases as people can no longer wear sandals in the cold weather (high demand).

High demand = higher price

How does this apply to share prices on the stock exchange?

Changes in the demand for shares affects the price of shares as well – either positively or negatively.

What causes the change in investor sentiment on the stock market?

Information. Information. INFORMATION.

The price of a share can go up because of speculation even if the actual operations and income generating capacity of the company have not changed. This is the power of speculation and is driven by information being priced into the market. This is why I love the stock market - it is unpredictable - and therein lies its treasure.

The interplay of these 3 factors – growth in business, inflation and speculation will affect the value of a share.

d) How does investing in shares actually grow your money?

One should note that investing your money in general causes an increase in the value of your money.

Firyal Hussain

Money grows as a result of 3 factors –

a) The capital invested – this is the amount that you are going to save
b) The rate of return – this is the expected percentage increase in your investment (example the interest rate on your bank savings account)
c) Period of time – this is how long you are going to be leaving your money in the investment

I am now going to explore a range of examples to help you to understand the impact of investing your money – bear in mind that these examples are hypothetical and are used for illustration purposes only.

Investment 1:

Assuming our investment amount is R6,000 per annum (p.a.), the interest rate that we will use is 3.5%:

Say for example that you saved R6,000 once off for the next 10 years in a bank account that offers an interest rate of 3.5% p.a. The interest compounding capability can be viewed in Table 1:

a) Capital invested = R6,000 once off
b) Rate of return = 3.5% p.a. (interest rate offered by the bank)
c) Period of time = 10 years

In 10 years' time, your R6,000 would have increased to R8,177.00.

Explanation of the calculation:

Year 3 = 6,210 + (3.5% * 6,210) = 6,427
Year 4 = 6,427 + (3.5% * 6,427) = 6,652
Year 5 = 6,652 + (3.5% * 6,652) = 6,885
Etc., etc.

This is the power of saving.

Year	Investment 1
1	6 000
2	6 210
3	6 427
4	6 652
5	6 885
6	7 126
7	7 376
8	7 634
9	7 901
10	8 177

Table 1

Investment 2:

Say for example that you are able to save R6,000 p.a. for the next 10 years in a bank account that offers an interest rate of 3.5% per annum. The interest compounding capability can be viewed in Table 2:

a) Capital invested = R6,000 per annum
b) Rate of return = 3.5% p.a. (interest rate offered by the bank)
c) Period of time = 10 years

In 10 years' time, your R6,000 p.a. would have increased to R70,388. If you remove the capital investment of R60,000 the accumulated interest amounts to R10,388.

Explanation of the calculation:

Year 3 = 12,210 + (3.5% * 12,210) + 6,000 = 18,637
Year 4 = 18,637 + (3.5% * 18,637) + 6,000 = 25,290
Year 5 = 25,290 + (3.5% * 25,290) + 6,000 = 32,175
Etc., etc.

Year	Investment 1	Investment 2	Capital investment 2 (6000*no of years)	Profit (Investment 1 less capital investment)	Profit (Investment 2 less capital investment)
1	6 000	6 000	6 000	-	-
2	6 210	12 210	12 000	210	210
3	6 427	18 637	18 000	427	637
4	6 652	25 290	24 000	652	1 290
5	6 885	32 175	30 000	885	2 175
6	7 126	39 301	36 000	1 126	3 301
7	7 376	46 676	42 000	1 376	4 676
8	7 634	54 310	48 000	1 634	6 310
9	7 901	62 211	54 000	1 901	8 211
10	8 177	70 388	60 000	2 177	10 388

Table 2

Capital investment = R6,000 per annum multiplied by the number of years (this is the amount that you physically put into the bank account per annum)

Interest made = Investment 2 minus capital investment (this is the interest that you have earned due to investing your money in the bank account)

In much the same way, you can invest your money on the JSE in the form of investing in shares. Investing in shares is riskier than investing in a bank account because your return is not guaranteed as it would be with a bank savings account.

This means that if you invest your money in a bank account, you would be guaranteed your 3.5% p.a. interest return (provided that the country's banks stay afloat). If you invest your money in shares, you are not guaranteed for example a 6% p.a. return. In fact, you may even experience negative returns! On the upside, you may receive a return that is greater than the 3.5% p.a. return offered by the bank over a period of time.

Articles show that the rate of return over a 5 and 10 year period are higher than that which can be earned in a bank account - the rate of return over a 10 year period can be as high as an average of 7.8% p.a. on the JSE.

The word average is operative here because one year could have provided -6% p.a. return and the next year could have provided a +25% p.a. return followed by a year of +1.6% p.a. return increase. Note that the average is significantly higher than interest rates offered by the banks.

Stock markets offer a higher **potential** rate of return over a period of time than an investment in a bank account. Potential – not guaranteed. This makes the investment in stocks/shares more risky than saving in a bank account.

Take a look at how the figures change with the higher rate of return on the JSE as compared to the bank interest rate (Table 3):

Assuming all other variables are the same, the rate of return is now 7.8% p.a.

a) Capital invested – Investment 1 = R6,000 once off
    Investment 2 = R6,000 per annum
b) Rate of return = 7.8% p.a. as mentioned above
c) Period of time = 10 years

Year	Investment 1	Investment 2	Capital investment 2 (6000*no of years)	Profit (Investment 1 less capital investment)	Profit (Investment 2 less capital investment)
1	6 000	6 000	6 000	-	-
2	6 468	12 468	12 000	468	468
3	6 973	19 441	18 000	973	1441
4	7 516	26 957	24 000	1 516	2 957
5	8 103	35 059	30 000	2 103	5 059
6	8 735	43 794	36 000	2 735	7 794
7	9 416	53 210	42 000	3 416	11 210
8	10 150	63 360	48 000	4 150	15 360
9	10 942	74 303	54 000	4 942	20 303
10	11 796	86 098	60 000	5 796	26 098

Table 3

The R6,000 once off becomes R11,796 in 10 years at 7.8% p.a. average rate of return on the JSE.

The total profit over and above the capital investment is R26,089 over 10 years where R6,000 is invested per annum instead of once off is more than double of that earned in a bank account over the same period of time.

This is why the stock market is a relevant investment tool for entrepreneurs. As an entrepreneur, you could take your money and invest it in a bank account where your interest return is almost guaranteed. Instead, you opted to invest in your business which could turn out to be a success or failure. You are already exhibiting the characteristics of a share investor!

Past to present performance of the JSE:

Over a period of 10 years to 18 Mar 2016, the JSE All Share Index has increased by 169.24%.

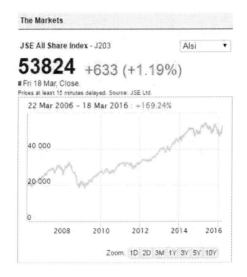

http://www.sharedata.co.za/

Graph 1

This means that if you invested R1.00 ten years ago, your R1.00 would be worth R2.69 today.

Calculation = R1 + R1 * 169.24% = R2.69

This may not seem like much, but if my mother had invested a once off R10,000 on the JSE for me ten years ago, that would be worth R26,924.00 today. Imagine if she had continued to invest a standard amount over the years, I would have been a very happy 18-year-old at the time.

Note that this 169.24% increase over the past 10 years was made up of a number of ups and downs. My lecturer once explained to me that investing on the stock market is like being in a relationship. You can't jump ship when the going gets rough.

A simple example is the performance of the JSE over the past year:

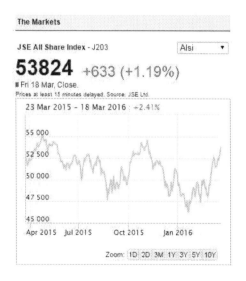

http://www.sharedata.co.za/

Graph 2

The picture is much more erratic and it is difficult to see whether there is an overall rise or fall in the value of your investment over a shorter period of time. Therefore, give your investment time to make money for you.

In much the same way, you would not close your new business venture that you have been toiling at for 17 months because you happen to have a rough patch. You stick it out and reap the rewards in the end.

e) Let's look at how to read the everyday stock market data

I found it challenging to understand what the different terms used to explain market data means at first. I have therefore produced screenshots from a popular website Sharenet.com which is South African based.

Below you will find extracts from the Sharenet.com website. I have attempted to explain what the different terms mean so that you may use them as a reference when looking at the data yourself.

Note that the terms may vary slightly from website to website but all provide the same fundamental data.

A spot price means the price that the item is valued at right now. Delayed spot prices by 15 minutes means that the website is reflecting a spot price that prevailed 15 minutes ago. You usually have to pay a monthly fee to obtain 100% live price feeds.

When looking to invest long-term, the importance of 100% live spot prices loses its importance – therefore information that you find freely on the internet (such as Google Finance) is perfect for you to utilise for share analysis.

Below is an extract of information showing the World Market Summary, JSE indexes, metal and forex spot prices. I have explained what the headings mean and these can be applied across the different items listed in the table below: http://www.sharenet.co.za/v3/spot.php

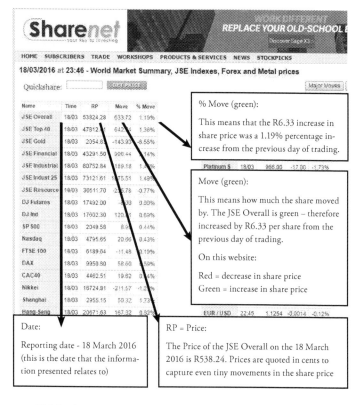

Table 4

The blue items above (the first 7 lines starting with the word "JSE") are JSE related results. If you are curious about what the remainder of the indices mean, I have completed a quick reference table for you:

Name of Indices	Short description
DJ Futures	America – Dow Jones Futures
DJ Ind	America – Dow Jones industrial index
SP 500	America – 500 largest companies on Nasdaq and NYSE
Nasdaq	American stock exchange
FTSE 100	London – share index of 100 companies on London Stock Exchange
DAX	Germany – 30 major German companies trading on Frankfurt Stock Exchange
CAC 40	France – 40 most significant companies on French Stock Market
Nikkei	Japan – Japanese Stock Market Index
Shanghai	China – Chinese Stock Market Index
Hang-Seng	Hong Kong – Top companies index of the Hong Kong Stock Exchange

The below table represents the major moves up and major moves down on the JSE for a specific day of trading – i.e. the 18 March 2016. I have explained what each of the headings mean using PIKWIK as an example.

Note that the % Move is ordered from highest to lowest for your convenience.

http://www.sharenet.co.za/v3/moves.php

Table 5

If you click on the hyperlink for PIKWIK in the table above, the site takes you to the following page which provides additional information relating to the share. I have explained the meaning behind each of these:

Note that all this information is freely available on the site. http://www.sharenet.co.za/v3/quickshare.php?scode=PWK

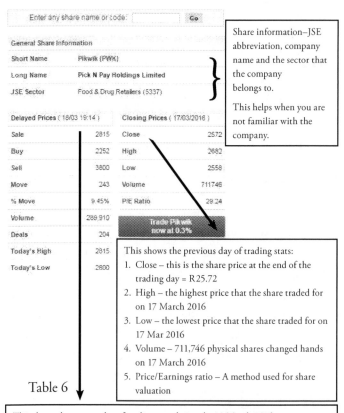

Share information–JSE abbreviation, company name and the sector that the company belongs to.

This helps when you are not familiar with the company.

This shows the previous day of trading stats:

1. Close – this is the share price at the end of the trading day = R25.72
2. High – the highest price that the share traded for on 17 March 2016
3. Low – the lowest price that the share traded for on 17 Mar 2016
4. Volume – 711,746 physical shares changed hands on 17 March 2016
5. Price/Earnings ratio – A method used for share valuation

Table 6

This shows the current day of trading stats being the 18 March 2016:

1. Sale – this means that the last sale happened at a price of R28.15 (a price that the seller and buyer agreed upon)
2. Buy – this is the price potential buyers are willing to buy a share at (buyers would want the lowest price to get the most value for their money)
3. Sell – this is the price potential sellers are willing to sell their shares at (sellers would want the highest price to make the highest profit)
4. Note – when the buyer and seller agree on a price, this is when the transaction actually takes place
5. Move and % Move – share price increased by R2.43 which is 9.45% from the previous day of trading (243 divided by 2572 *100 = 9.45%)
6. Volume – the number of shares traded so far on 18 March 2016 is 289,910 shares
7. Deals – the number of transactions. There were 204 transactions (of buy and sell) which resulted in 289,910 shares changing hands
8. Today's High - the highest price that the share traded for thus far on 18 March 2016
9. Today's Low – the lowest price that the share traded for thus far on 18 Mar 2016

SENS news

SENS is the real-time Stock Exchange News which publishes price sensitive information to the public. This type of information could affect investor sentiment and cause speculation which would affect share prices.

SENS news is free on the internet; you may even check this out on the Sharenet.com website.

f) Is the stock market a reflection of the economy?

The answer to this is both yes and no.

If you have managed to come this far, I take my hat off to you – you need only read the next chapter and my work here is done.

We have come to the climax of the book – this is where we step away from the miniscule detail and try to understand the broader context of what I am trying to help you to understand about the stock market.

When do economies grow?

-   Economies grow when there is increased productivity and efficiency in companies – think of reducing fixed costs and improving productivity methods
-   Economies grow when consumer goods and services are more readily available to more people – think of the impact of internet access to people in rural areas in Africa and the education opportunities this could bring about
-   Economies grow once people can buy what they need and still save – think of the impact on the economy

if people need to use debt to buy electricity and food each month

What is the impact of individuals saving?

- If you and I are able to save a percentage of our income each month, these savings can filter into the stock and bond market either directly or indirectly
- Directly = through you buying shares of Company S through an IPO using an online platform
- Indirectly = your pension fund invests 35% of funds in the equity market for example and the remainder in bonds
- Whether the company is selling bonds or shares, they are able to raise this capital by virtue of being listed or by listing on the stock exchange

What do companies do with funding received?

- Bonds are usually used by companies to cover overhead and operating costs – we will not focus on this in this assessment
- Long-term financing is usually obtained via share issues due to the long-term nature of shares

Example – Company A has now successfully acquired Company Q and intends to provide large amounts of capital to assist Company Q with the cancer treatment research and development. Company A decides to do a share issue to raise the necessary funds which it will invest in Company Q;

- Share issue funds received by Company A will be pumped into Company Q
- Share issues provide a cheaper means of raising finance as no interest is payable as is the case with debt – this means that Company A and Company Q have more money available to use on the research than if they had to make annual interest payments to the lender if money was raised through a loan
- With this money raised through the sale of shares, Company Q purchases assets and pays specialist companies to construct new assets necessary for the research and development of the product – this causes an increase in GDP
- Company Q employs more people to enable them to manage the increased workload – this is a mix of engineers, biochemists, secretaries, cleaning staff and bookkeepers – this increases employment figures in the economy

We can see from this that the stock exchange forms a part of the economy. There is a flow of money from you, to the listed company, which in turn leads to increased GDP and increased employment rates. Increased employment would mean generation of further economic activity by the new employees.

The impact of a bull market

In a bull market, share prices increase (think of a bull thrusting its horns towards the sky – this movement can be associated with increase).

If you own shares on the stock exchange, a bull market creates a wealth effect. This means that your investment is worth more which enables you to spend more on big items such as homes and motor vehicles – this in turn stimulates the economy.

Companies would generally reflect higher profits due to increased sales. Additional money would be available to invest in expansion projects and thereby employing more people to work on those projects.

Employment brings in more economic participants which will further increase consumer spending.

When there is a high demand for employees, packages are driven higher because candidates are in a better position negotiate better terms. This results in greater household savings.

A bull market creates confidence in the economy which results in greater investment on the stock market due to the now increased household savings - this further increases the price of shares.

The impact of a bear market

In a bear market, share prices decrease (think of a bear standing on its hind legs, then falling forward to rest on all fours – this movement can be associated with decrease).

If you own shares on the stock exchange, a bear market creates the opposite of a wealth effect. This means that what you have invested in shares is now worth less because of the decreasing share prices. This would cause people to hold back on spending which would then slow down economic growth.

If you and I spend less, companies receive less revenue for expansion which impacts GDP. If revenue keeps decreasing, companies look to restructuring in order to reduce headcount in an attempt to keep the business afloat. This then impacts unemployment rates.

If more people are unemployed, more people have to eat into their savings (sell off shares) and use debt to cover their living expenses.

A bear market creates a pessimistic outlook for all and investors tend to sell off their shares in search of a safer investment such as a bank savings account for example.

If investors pull out of the stock market, and the price of shares continues to fall.

The media can sometimes fast track this by creating a panic when share prices begin to fall.

Note – this is a great time to invest in shares as share prices are generally low, and catching them at this price would be a bargain!

Conclusion:

The stock market forms a part of the economy. The actions of one can impact the other and vice versa. It is a mix of economic growth, investor sentiment, consumer spending, funding received by large corporates, inflation, construction, development and employment. We would be unable to separate the stock market from the economy.

g) What costs are involved buying and selling shares (remember what I said – *need to know basis*)

(This information is as at 25 Mar 2016, you may check the updated fees online or contact your broker to find out if anything has changed).

As an entrepreneur, you understand the importance of knowing the costs involved before plunging into a business transaction.

Buying and selling of shares on the stock exchange is no different. I will therefore introduce you to the types of fees you can expect when buying and selling shares here on the JSE in South Africa.

In order to buy and sell shares, you will need to open a brokerage account because the JSE does not sell shares directly to the public. Brokerage accounts can come in many forms such as:

1. Share trading account with a bank
2. An account with an actual brokerage firm
3. An account with an online trading platform

No matter the type of account you open, you will have fees to pay.

Fixed fees associated with your brokerage account –

The brokerage will charge you a fixed admin fee per month. This fee can be waivered if you for example trade in shares more than 5 times in a month. Reason – brokerage firms make a commission on your trading transactions. The more you trade, the more commission they make which is why they are able to waiver the fixed fee if your account has a lot of activity.

Variable costs associated with your brokerage account – called brokerage/commissions

The broker will charge you a % on the value of shares in a transaction – transaction cost. The majority of brokerage firms will charge you a transaction fee and a commission fee on a sliding scale.

How much effort should I put into choosing the right brokerage account? –

I implore you to spend a long time investigating different brokerage accounts before making your decision on what is best for you. Reason being that it would be the account that you would be using for the foreseeable future.

It would not be wise to switch after having made investments with a specific broker because it costs you money to move your shares between brokerage accounts. You could open a second account, but that would mean that you would be paying monthly fees on 2 or more brokerage accounts which you could rather use towards your investment.

What can I expect when researching different broker accounts? – As mentioned above, there are fixed and variable costs associated with a brokerage account.

1. There would be a fixed admin fee which can be waived if you trade more than x times in a specified period of time
2. There would be a minimum commission and a commission calculated as a percentage of any transactions you enter into (the fee would be the higher of the 2 commissions)
3. You can also expect there to be a minimum account size for some brokers

Here is a list of real life fees that you can expect (information as at July 2016):

Broker	Minimum commission (excl. VAT)	Commission (excl. VAT)	Admin fee	Minimum account size
Sharenet Securities	R110	0.3%	R200 quarterly (waived if you trade 4 times or more in the quarter)	R50,000
ABSA	R120 (or R0 for private bankers)	0.4%	R66.66 per month (waived if you trade 5 times or more in the year)	R0
FNB Securities	R100	0.5%	R70 per month	R25,000
Sanlam	R75	0 – R500,000 = R75 plus 0.5% R500,001 to R1m = 0.4% Above R1m = 0.35%	R50 per month (waived if brokerage fee is more than R300 in the month)	R1,000
Standard Bank	R80	0.5%	R80 per month (waived if you trade 3 times or more in the month)	R0

You may use a similar format when performing your own analysis and add more criteria if you like. A good idea is to make a list of what you are looking for and assess each account based on this criterion.

Other charges:

JSE costs:

STRATE fee -

STRATE is our South African Central Securities Depository (CSD) which is trusted to promote the efficiency and safety of the financial markets.

STRATE therefore charges fees for the trading of shares. You will pay STRATE fees when <u>buying and selling</u> shares.

1. *On market settlement fee –*
   R14.94 per transaction leg (incl. VAT) [R13.10 excl. VAT)
2. *Contract Note Fee –*

Details	Amount incl. VAT	Amount excl. VAT
Transaction up to R200,000	R13.20	R11.58
Transaction greater than R200,000 but less than R1mil	0.006597% of transaction value	0.005787% of transaction value
Transaction value is greater than R1mil	R65.97	R57.87

Insider Protection Levy (IPL) –

This levy is paid when you buy and sell stocks and is used to fund investigations into market manipulation and insider trading.

This levy is 0.0002% of the purchase price of shares. Hence you only pay this levy when <u>buying</u> shares.

What is insider trading?

Insider trading happens when a person who has confidential information (information not readily available to the public) and uses it to his/her advantage on the stock market.

For example, Mr T works for a listed company, Company Funding Ltd. He is called into a board meeting to provide expert advice on the possibility of merger with a powerful competitor, Company Talent Ltd. Mr T provides his expert advice and the board decides to go ahead with the merger.

Mr T knows that once this information becomes public, the price of both companies will soar. He quickly calls up his wife and tells her to buy X amount of shares in Company Funding Ltd while he buys shares in Company Talent Ltd.

In this case both Mr T and his wife will have been involved in insider trading.

This is a very basic example but it explains the just of what insider trading is.

Why is insider trading so bad?

Insider trading is a branch of the root of discrimination. The individuals who have access to information of this caliber, represent a minority. Being allowed to use this information to their benefit would put the poor majority at a further disadvantage in the stock market arena.

Given South Africa's past, we know all too well the impact of discrimination on society. In terms of the Financial Markets Act 2012 s78, an insider trader commits an offence when he has insider information and acts on directly/indirectly to his benefit.

Government levies and taxes:

Securities Transfer Tax –

A tax on the transfer of securities (such as equity shares).

The current charge is 0.25% of the total purchase price. This means that you only pay this on the <u>purchase</u> of shares.

VAT –

VAT of 14% is charged on the brokerage fee, STRATE costs and the IPL.

Capital Gains Tax –

If you hold the shares as a long term investment, tax is payable upon the sale of shares if you have made a profit. A percentage of this profit will be taxed as part of your annual tax return.

Note that if you are a speculator i.e. you buy and sell shares for short term profit and not for long term investment, your full profit will be taxed.

Summary –

When buying shares, you are not just paying the purchase price of shares. There are a host of other costs which you should be wary of. While the brokerage costs may vary slightly from broker to broker, there are some costs which cannot be avoided.

There are South African sites online which can even calculate the total cost of your transaction using an online share trading calculator – FOR FREE! I found this by simply typing "online share trading calculator" in a popular search engine.

h) As an entrepreneur, how does this apply to you?

Get educated

There are too many articles and books out there which claim to know a recipe for share trading which will result in instant riches.

As a business person, you know that building a business requires endless hours of hard and smart work. Stock trading is no different. Given the raw talent for learning only what is important, entrepreneurs should acquire the skills required to invest in shares because, like business, the stock exchange is an avalanche of opportunity ready for the taking.

The internet provides a staggering amount of free information on companies that are listed on the stock exchange to enable you to practice your skills even if you will not have accumulated enough cash to invest for the next few years. (I came across mountains of free training content (videos and online courses) on the JSE website which would be a good place to start). Once you have a good grip on what methods you would like to use, you can start trying them out using free platforms such as Google Finance.

If you are serious about learning more on the stock exchange, Sharenet.com holds nationwide educational seminars and boasts the longest published stock market course (which includes exams).

You can become more relevant and upbeat starting from today with current market information through 2 main radio shows; Lindsay Williams' Fine Business Daily (FBR) and The Moneyweb show - The Money Talk on Radio 2000. Both these shows happen at 6pm, you can listen to one and catch up on the podcast of the other if you like.

The JSE has 2 listing platforms – the Main Board and the AltX.

The Main Board

More than 400 companies are listed on the JSE's Main Board which includes the JSE's Top 40 stocks. This is where you will find the large, mature companies such as MTN, Shoprite, Anglo American, Growthpoint, Capitec, etc.

The AltX

The AltX lists smaller companies which are high-growth and of a good quality. It enables these companies to obtain funding even though they are not large enough to list on the JSE.

As an entrepreneur, the AltX is a collection shares which are both possibly undervalued and very risky. Given that entrepreneurs are able to identify opportunity and have risk appetite that is unlike the average employee, the AltX is a good place to start looking for that first fiery share to invest in. Because these companies are high-growth, it may be that your share price could double within 3 years.

Risk also means that there could be a downside. This is applicable whether you invest in shares on the Main Board or the AltX.

My advice to you is to educate yourself on stocks and how to analyse them using the resources mentioned above.

1. How to pick shares

Decide on a portfolio that works for you.

The beauty of share investing is that you may invest in what is best for you. You could have a portfolio of Main Board shares and be on the lookout for AltX shares which you would invest in once you have made a thorough analysis.

Alternatively, you could invest in AltX shares alone.

Each person is different therefore we should all be comfortable with a different mix of share investments.

Instead of selecting specific shares, you could even opt to invest in ETF's or Exchange Traded Funds which are my personal favourite.

What is an ETF?

An ETF (exchange traded fund) is an instrument which tracks the movement of a group of shares, whatever that group may be. The group of shares that the ETF aims to track can be called *indices*.

A similitude is that of a classroom.

There are 10 children in the classroom writing a maths test. After the test, each child's mark would be different. Using the average of the class, you as a student can gauge whether you are performing above/below the average of the class.

In much the same way, the stock market is made up of individual shares (just like each child in a classroom). There is an overall performance of the stock market on a specific day (just like the average mark achieved in the maths test by the students in the class).

An ETF aims to track the overall performance of the stock market thereby encompassing the movement of a group of shares instead of a specific share (like the average math mark in the class).

An ETF can be purchased in the same way as an ordinary share and can be traded on the stock market just like an ordinary share.

ETFs are a great way to gain exposure to a range of shares – you are able to achieve a level of *portfolio diversification* (a share portfolio containing a mix of shares which reduces your overall risk) which a starting investor cannot obtain by investing in a few ordinary shares. It is an excellent investment tool for beginners who are unsure about choosing individual shares to invest in on the stock market.

The most attractive feature of an ETF is the cost thereof. Unlike a mutual fund which requires active management by a fund manager, an ETF does not require management of any sort (because it simply mimics the average of an index) which makes it cheaper. In addition, there is no need for a sales intermediary because the ETF can be traded directly on the stock exchange like a normal share. Again, a cost cutter! Examples of what ETFs can track are:

1. Broad exposure – SATRIX 40
2. Sector exposure – SATRIX FINI (exposure to banks), SATRIX RESI (mining and resources)
3. Property – STANLIB Property
4. Dividend companies – SATRIX DIVI

There are many ETFs to consider, research the range of ETFs to get a full view of what is available to invest in.

Have you heard of the new JSE Tax-Free Savings Account (TFSA's)?

Here is some exciting news! The JSE now offers a new savings account for investing in ETFs.

The name explains what the account aims to achieve – no tax on activities associated with the account:

1. Interest earned – not taxed
2. Dividends earned – no dividend withholding tax charged
3. Profit made on sale – no capital gains tax charged
4. Purchases made – no securities transfer tax charged

The condition of this account is that you will need to invest in an ETF monthly/as a lump sum and there is a maximum of R500,000 lifetime contribution.

Extract from *The Intelligent Investor* by Benjamin Graham:

"In an article in a women's magazine many years ago we advised the readers to buy their stocks as they bought their groceries, not as they bought their perfume."

Shares should be bought when you believe that the share is undervalued. If it is undervalued, you would expect the share price to rise over a period of time. This makes it a potentially good investment.

The extract above explains that shares should not be bought simply because they are expensive. It is not like buying perfume or brand name shoes where the pricier, the better. You need to choose shares based on the reasonability of the share price – the more undervalued you think the share is, the more valuable the share becomes as an investment choice.

There are many methods to value shares, some are complex and others simple enough for novices to use as a base. You will come across the different types of share valuation methods by educating yourself on the subject.

Once you have educated yourself, you have done your research and you have found your first burning share that you would like to invest in, I say take the leap and go for it. I say this even though there is still so much that you may not know.

You cannot wait until you know 100% on the subject of share trading because that will never happen. In any event, you will never be 100% sure that your share is going to outperform and increase your investment value. The share price may actually go down despite your efforts!

It is important to note that even the experts can get it wrong – that is a comforting thought for me because no matter how complex your analysis might be, the share price will still have a mind of its own.

It can - and will - surprise you.

2. Standing the test of time

After buying your chosen share, hold on to it. Do not panic at the first sight of the share price dropping and sell up because this would mean that you bought the share at a high price and sold it at a low price – which makes zero business sense.

Once you buy the shares, step back. Give your chosen company time to prove itself. This is why I emphasise that live share prices are not extremely important; it represents the situation at a specific point in time. You should be more interested in the overall performance of the share since your purchase, daily movements are simply inputs to the bigger picture which is what you should be more interested in.

Check on the performance of your shares at intervals that you are comfortable with. I would suggest spending majority of your time on your business and minimal time checking the share prices of your shares once bought because you don't actually have to do anything to increase their value but wait. Your business on the other hand needs more of your valuable attention and time.

Hold onto your shares even if the world shrieks that the sky is falling!

CHAPTER 5

Closing

"It's not how much money you make, but how much money you keep, how hard it works for you, and how many generations you keep it for."

Robert Kiyosaki

I will leave you with the reasoning behind my title of this book: "Sell yourself short!"

I would like to use these last few minutes to make your brain work for you:

Suppose you and I are sharing a sandwich at the Walter Sisulu Botanical Gardens. We are sitting under the tree on the bench facing the relaxing waterfall.

I am your stock broker and you are my client (just before you start thinking that this was going to get romantic).

The sound of the water hitting the rocks and the shadow of the eagle soaring above electrifies a few short circuits in your grey matter and you express an unusual proposal.

You believe that the share price of Company XXX is going to go down.

You ask me to borrow you 100 shares of XXX from the brokerage in order to sell these on the open market.

I agree.

You take the 100 shares and you sell them all within 3 days at R165.00 per share. Your brokerage account has therefore increased by R16,500.00 from the sale of the borrowed shares.

Eventually, you need to return my shares to me (I agreed a period of 7 days with you).

You wait 4 more days and buy the shares at R154.20 per share.

Net impact of the transaction on your account:

Sale of shares that you borrowed	R16,500.00
Purchase of shares to return to me	(R15,420.00)
Net impact	R 1,080.00 profit

You made R1,080.00 profit from absolutely nothing but opportunity identification and execution of your brilliant plan.

In just 7 days' time, you are R1,080.00 richer and I have my shares back!

The term used for the above is to "have a short position in share XXX".

You held a short position in the stock because you had borrowed the shares from me temporarily expecting the share price to fall – and expecting to make a profit therefrom.

The term "Don't sell yourself short" means don't underestimate your abilities. Selling short in share trading as explained above could mean exploiting an opportunity.

Therefore instead of following the saying "Don't sell yourself short", I say;

Sell yourself short!

and go make some money...

ABOUT THE AUTHOR

The author is a qualified finance professional with a passion for the stock market. With a background of informal tutoring, she has developed a simplistic flair to explaining complex concepts in an easy-to-understand language.

Credentials – Bachelor of Accounting Science (Honours) University of the Witwatersrand 2011; Finance Professional, Germinating Entrepreneur, Digger-of-Gold

ABOUT THE BOOK

This is an excellent book for anyone intending to understand what the stock market is and how it works with a clearly defined focus on educating entrepreneurs.

This book takes a step by step approach in teaching you what the stock market is and how it operates - in a proudly South African context.

Although focusing on the JSE, the fundamentals of share value and investor sentiment are echoed across the stock markets throughout the world.

Come explore!

Why do I want to learn about the stock market?

_____

_____

_____

_____

_____

_____

_____

_____

_____

_____

_____

_____

_____

_____

_____

_____

_____

_____

_____

_____

_____

_____

_____

_____

Stuff to research further

_____
_____
_____
_____
_____
_____
_____
_____
_____
_____
_____
_____
_____
_____
_____
_____
_____
_____
_____
_____
_____
_____
_____
_____
_____
_____

Important points to remember going forward

_____

_____

_____

_____

_____

_____

_____

_____

_____

_____

_____

_____

_____

_____

_____

_____

_____

_____

_____

_____

_____

_____

_____

_____

_____

_____